IMMIGRATION

Fina's Story
From Mexico to Texas

By Sarah Glasscock
Illustrated by Neil Reed

PICTURE CREDITS
Page backgrounds © Digital Vision/Getty Images; 4 Mapping Specialists, Ltd.; 5 (top) © Robert Frerck/Getty Images; 5 (bottom) © Adalberto Rios Szalay/Sexto Sol/Photodisc/Getty Images; 60 © Hulton Archive/Getty Images; 61 © Time Life Pictures/Getty Images; 62 (top) © Bob Krist/Corbis; 62 (bottom) © Reuters/Corbis; 64 © Trevor Wood/Getty Images.

PUBLISHED BY THE NATIONAL GEOGRAPHIC SOCIETY
Produced through the worldwide resources of the National Geographic Society, John M. Fahey, Jr., President and Chief Executive Officer; Gilbert M. Grosvenor, Chairman of the Board.

PREPARED BY NATIONAL GEOGRAPHIC SCHOOL PUBLISHING
Sheron Long, Chief Executive Officer; Samuel Gesumaria, President; Francis Downey, Vice President and Publisher; Richard Easby, Editorial Manager; Anne M. Stone, Editor; Margaret Sidlosky, Director of Design and Illustrations; Jim Hiscott, Design Manager; Cynthia Olson, Ruth Ann Thompson, Art Directors; Matt Wascavage, Director of Publishing Services; Lisa Pergolizzi, Production Manager.

MANUFACTURING AND QUALITY CONTROL
Christopher A. Liedel, Chief Financial Officer; Phillip L. Schlosser, Vice President; Clifton M. Brown III, Director.

CONSULTANT
Mary Anne Wengel

BOOK DESIGN
Artful Doodlers and Insight Design Concepts Ltd.

Copyright © 2007 National Geographic Society. All Rights Reserved. Reproduction of the whole or any part of the contents without written permission is prohibited. National Geographic, National Geographic Reading Expeditions, and the Yellow Border are registered trademarks of the National Geographic Society.

Published by the National Geographic Society
1145 17th Street N.W.
Washington, D.C. 20036-4688

Product #4U1005084
ISBN: 978-1-4263-5077-1

Printed in Mexico

11 10 09 08 07
10 9 8 7 6 5 4 3 2 1

CONTENTS

The Setting 4

The Characters 6

Chapter 1 Fina Speaks Up 9

Chapter 2 Changes Ahead 18

Chapter 3 Trouble in Puebla 33

Chapter 4 The Journey 40

Chapter 5 The Letter 50

The Facts Behind the Story 60

Read, Research, and Write 63

Extend Your Reading 64

THE SETTING

Leaving home

The United States is a nation of immigrants. These are people who have moved to a new place, leaving the country where they were born. Some people have come to escape from wars, conflict, or hunger at home. Others have come to find freedom and new opportunities. Whatever the reason, this country has grown thanks to waves of immigrants. One of these waves came from Mexico around 1910.

Mexico

Geography Mexico is a country south of the United States. It is about three times the size of Texas. The landscape varies from tropical forests to rugged mountains, deserts, and even volcanoes. Mexico is rich in natural resources like oil, silver, gold, copper, and coal.

The People Most Mexicans have roots in two cultures, Spanish and native. Today more than two-thirds of Mexicans live in cities. In fact, Mexico City is one of the largest cities in the world. Mexican factories make cars, clothing, appliances, and other products. Fishing is also a major industry. Farmers grow corn, wheat, rice, beans, coffee, cotton, and fruit.

THE CHARACTERS

THE RECIO FAMILY

Josefina
"Fina" is eleven years old. She dreams that someday she will be able to go to school and learn to read and write. But there is no school where she and her family live.

Raul
Fina's father is a farmer. His family once owned the land they lived on, but it was taken away by the government. Now it is owned by a wealthy man. Raul Recio works for the owner.

Blanca
Blanca is Teresa's twin sister. She lives on another hacienda. She feels close to her sister, but only sees her a few times a year.

Teresa
Fina's mother grows corn, beans, and squash in a small garden to feed her family. She also earns money by sewing blouses with colorful designs. She sells them in the nearby city of Puebla.

Marcos
Fina's brother, Marcos, is sixteen. When he is not working in the cornfields, he loves to play baseball.

CHAPTER 1

Fina Speaks Up

Fina Recio hid among the tall plants in the cornfield. The corn had been harvested, and some ears were roasting in a nearby pit. The smell made Fina's stomach rumble, but not only because she was hungry. She was nervous too. She had an important question for Señor Vega. Would he listen? If he did, would he say yes?

As they did every spring, the people who worked on Señor Vega's hacienda were celebrating the harvesting of the corn. The hacienda was a large plantation, or farm. It was spread over thousands of acres of land in central Mexico. A few people, like Fina's parents, lived on small farms on the hacienda. Others worked in the cornfields. At the center of the hacienda were Señor Vega's huge country house, a church, a store, and even a baseball field. The only thing missing was a school.

Suddenly, Fina heard the crack of a bat. A baseball flew over her head and fell into the middle of the field.

Two men rushed past Fina to search for the baseball. "Is the game over?" Fina asked when the men returned empty-handed.

One of the men nodded. "*Sí*, Marcos Recio just hit a homerun to win the game."

Fina jumped up and down and clapped. Her brother, Marcos, had hit a homerun! His team had won. This was a good sign. Two years ago, Marcos had been able to talk Señor Vega into building the baseball field. Today, on April 15, 1910, Fina would talk the *señor* into building a school for the hacienda.

She ran to her mother, who was laughing and clapping. "*¡Viva Marcos!*" she called. "Long live Marcos!"

"Mama—don't you think Marcos is the best baseball player in all of Mexico?" Fina asked.

Teresa Recio smoothed her daughter's dark hair. "Josefina Recio, how did you get mud on your face? You looked so nice when we left home."

Fina tried to stand still while her mother fussed over her hair and clothes. She wanted to look her best when she talked to Señor Vega.

"Look at your blouse!" Teresa scolded. "Do you know how many hours it took for me to make it? Do you know how much money I could have sold it for at the market in Puebla?"

Fina felt terrible about getting her blouse dirty. Her mother had worked on it at night after working all day long in their *milpas*—their family's garden of corn, squash, and beans.

"Señor Vega has promised to give five *centavos* to each player on the winning team," Fina said.

"We can use the money," her mother replied. "The price of seeds at the hacienda store is going up. It has been a bad year—not enough rain, not enough corn."

Fina wondered how much money it would take to build and run a school. Maybe today wasn't the best day to ask for it. She shook her head until her braids slapped her shoulders, trying to decide.

No—it had to be today. Tomorrow, Señor Vega would go back to Mexico City, where he lived with his family. The workers only saw Señor Vega when it was time to harvest the corn. Besides, other haciendas had schools. Fina wanted to learn to read and write. She wanted to learn about the rest of Mexico and the world.

Teresa caught her daughter's head in her hands. "Fina! Why are you shaking your head like that? Go and get an ear of corn from your father."

Fina headed for the edge of the cornfield where her father, Raul, and the other men were pulling corn out of the fire pit. The coals turned the cornhusks dry and brown, but the corn inside was juicy. When her father

squeezed lime juice on the corn, the juice sizzled from the heat. Then he sprinkled chili powder on the corn—just the way Fina liked it.

Of course, her father had to give the first ear of hot corn to Señor Vega. After all, it was his land and his corn.

The *señor* raised the ear of corn and smiled. He barely nibbled the corn and then wiped his mouth with a white handkerchief. "The corn is sweet, but not as sweet as it was last year," he said, handing the ear of corn back to Raul. After cleaning his fingers, he reached into his coat pocket. "Where are the winners of the baseball game?"

The players on the winning team waved their hands. "Here! Here, *señor!*"

Fina could hear the coins jingling in Señor Vega's palm. This was her chance. "Señor Vega!" she spoke up. "Could we use the money to build a school instead?"

Señor Vega laughed. He tossed the coins into the air and caught them again. "Who wants to give their money to start a school?" he asked. "Raise your hands!"

Nobody raised his hand—not even Marcos. Fina couldn't believe it. "Marcos, raise your hand!" she said to her brother.

"This is your daughter, Raul?" Señor Vega asked. "How old is she?"

Fina felt her father's hands tighten slightly on her shoulders, a warning. "Hush, Fina," he whispered.

She couldn't stop herself. She had to find the right words to convince Señor Vega. "My name is Josefina Recio, and I'm eleven years old. You have children, *señor,*" she continued. "They go to school, don't they? They live in Mexico City, and they go to school there?"

"Yes, of course, my children go to school," Señor Vega answered proudly. "They speak Spanish, English, and French." He shook his finger at Fina. "But you have no need for school. Your mother and your father will teach you everything you need to know. Your mother will teach you how to cook and sew. Your father will teach you how to grow corn and raise chickens. I'm sure they'll teach you how to speak with respect to the people you work for."

Señor Vega got on his horse. The noon sun blazed on the silver on the heavy saddle and stirrups. Before he rode away, he threw the coins into the air. "If you want them, you must catch them!" he said.

Almost everyone tried to catch a coin. Men dived to grab the money as it hit the ground. Some of them started fighting over the money. Raul held Marcos back.

"But that's my money, Papa!" Marcos protested. "My team won. We earned it!"

"If you do a good job and you earn the money, then you shouldn't have to fight over it in the dirt," Raul told his son. "That's not right."

Fina couldn't believe how quickly the celebration had ended. There would be no five-*centavo* piece to take home. There would be no school.

Everyone was quiet on the ride home. From the back of the donkey cart, Fina watched gray clouds roll over Popocatepetl. They looked like clouds of ash rising from the cone of the volcano. Fina liked to repeat the full name of the volcano over and over again, faster and faster: "PO-PO-CA-TE-PET-AL, PO-PO-CA-TE-PET-AL, PO-PO-CA-TE-PET-AL." Señor Vega probably thought he owned Popo too.

If they lived on another hacienda or in Mexico City or the United States, she wouldn't be able to see Popo through her window in the morning. She would miss that. But if they moved somewhere else, she might be able to go to school. Fina knew she would prefer learning over almost anything else. Life just didn't seem fair to Fina. Why couldn't she go to school?

When the cart bumped to a stop in front of their little house, Fina climbed out. She went into the yard to feed the chickens. Except for the scratching and pecking of the chickens, it seemed so quiet. It was like being in her own private world. At home, she could pretend that the house was not part of Señor Vega's hacienda. Instead she pretended that they owned the house that her father had built himself.

The walls of the house were sturdy and thick. Her father had mixed mud and hay and then packed it into wooden boxes to dry into **adobe** bricks. Inside the house, he'd smoothed mud over the bricks. Every spring, they whitewashed the walls with lime. This is our house because we love it, Fina thought. But she knew in her heart that it wasn't really theirs.

Her father led the donkey into the corral at the back of the house. Fina tossed the grain and kept her eyes on the ground. "I'm sorry about the money, Papa," she said, trying to keep her voice steady. "It's my fault that Marcos didn't bring home the five *centavos.*"

Raul spread hay for the donkey. "I know how much you want to go to school. You should be able to get an

---
adobe – a thick clay made into bricks and used for building

education. But it won't do any good to ask Señor Vega." He smiled sadly at his daughter and looked away.

Fina knew her father was right. If a tool broke, he tried to fix it so he wouldn't have to go to the hacienda store and buy another one. The store charged too much money. Tears dripped down Fina's cheeks and hit the dirt like raindrops. "How will things ever change?" she asked.

Raul wiped the tears from Fina's face. "Things do change," he told her. "You know that my grandparents owned this land once. Then President Diaz said Señor Vega could take their land. One day, someone else will be president of Mexico. Who knows? He might give the land back to us—and to all the other people whose land has been taken from them."

"But what if nothing changes?" Fina asked.

Kneeling down, Raul looked at Fina. "You're going to go to school, Fina," he promised. "I don't know how, but you will."

The rich smell of chilis, chocolate, cinnamon, and other spices came from inside the house. Her mother was making *mole* sauce to celebrate the day. Fina sighed in happiness and focused on her father's words. One day, she would go to school.

CHAPTER 2

Changes Ahead

Early the next morning, Fina tried to keep her eyes open as she got dressed. It was still very dark outside, and even the chickens and the rooster were asleep. But today was market day in Puebla, and the family had to leave early. The large city was 15 kilometers from their house. It would take them several hours to reach it.

All Fina had to do was stay awake long enough to walk outside and get into the donkey cart. Her mother always made her a comfortable bed of striped blankets in the cart. Once her head hit the blankets, Fina could sleep until they reached Puebla. But just the thought of the soft blankets made her fall back into her real bed. She didn't wake when her father carried her out and gently placed her in the back of the cart. She didn't even wake up when the donkey bucked and made the cart jolt down the dirt road. When Fina finally did wake up, they were in Puebla.

CHANGES AHEAD

The cart bumped up and down on the cobblestone streets of the old city. They passed houses with black iron fences that looked like lace. Some houses had beautiful tiles on the front. Fina wanted to live in a house with tiles one day. It was just one more thing she dreamed of doing.

The sun was just coming up, but the market square was already full of people selling and buying things. Rows of pots and tiles lined the square. They were white and painted with blue and sometimes other colors like green and yellow. *Poblanos,* the people of Puebla, were famous for the pottery and tiles they made.

Fina loved coming to Puebla. People from all over the world visited the city. They bought beautiful white blouses from her mother. Along the square necks of the blouses, her mother had sewn beautiful patterns with different colors of thread—red and blue, purple and green, black and yellow. Her blouses were traditional, but they were also unique.

Settling into their usual place in the northeastern corner of the square, the Recios waved to the other sellers. Fina helped her mother place the blouses on a blanket. Marcos filled a large straw basket with cornhusk dolls, while his father hung braids of garlic and peppers from their garden.

FINA'S STORY

Fina spotted one of her favorite tour guides. He took Mexicans, Americans, and Europeans all over Puebla and explained the city's history to them. Fina had listened to the guide so many times that she could understand some of what he said in English.

She waved to the guide. "Mama, may I go and say hello?" she asked. Maybe she'd learn some new English words today.

"You've heard his stories so many times. You could probably give your own tour of Puebla," Marcos joked. "Tell me this: When was the city of Puebla founded, my Señorita Recio?"

CHANGES AHEAD

"The Spanish built Puebla in 1531," Fina said. "It's one of the oldest cities in Mexico that the Spanish built."

"You should be the one giving tours. You should be charging all these rich people to tell them the history of Puebla," Marcos said.

Fina couldn't tell if Marcos was joking now or not. Giving tours sounded like a good idea to her. It would be a way to earn money for the family. If she listened really hard to the guide, she thought she'd even be able to give the tour in English.

"How much do you think the tourists would pay me?" she asked Marcos.

Marcos laughed. "I was kidding, Fina."

"I knew that," Fina scowled. She tried to hide her disappointment. She thought she'd make a good tour guide. She turned to her mother to ask again if she could say hello to the tour guide.

Her mother was standing on her tiptoes, searching the crowd of people in the plaza. Fina knew immediately who her mother was looking for: her twin sister Blanca. There were many women with their hair pinned back, wearing bright head scarves, **embroidered** white blouses, and skirts. But none of them was Blanca.

Fina put her arm around her mother's waist. "I hope we see Aunt Blanca today," she whispered. Her aunt lived on the other side of Puebla. She worked on another hacienda that was even larger than Señor Vega's. It had a school too. But that hacienda was at least 25 kilometers away from Puebla. They never knew when Blanca would be able to come to the market.

Teresa rubbed Fina's back. "I hope so too, Fina. I miss my sister so much," she sighed. "Come on, let's finish putting out the blouses."

A man stopped to buy some garlic. He often bought things from Fina's family. Today, the man shook Raul's hand. "I wanted to say goodbye." Then he held up the

---

embroidered – decorated with needlework designs

braid of garlic. "I'm taking this garlic to the United States with me. I don't think garlic in the United States will taste as good as yours does, Raul."

"It sounds like you're leaving Mexico," Raul replied.

"I am—at least for a while," the man said. "I've got a job at a coal mine outside of Laredo, Texas."

"They grow good Bermuda onions around Laredo," Raul told the man. "I hear they need workers there too."

"They also have a baseball team!" Marcos said excitedly. "They're called the Laredo Bermudas—after the onions!"

"Do they have schools there, Papa?" Fina asked. "If they do, maybe we should move to Laredo too."

A woman's voice came from behind them. "Fina Recio, why would you want to move?"

"Aunt Blanca!" Fina shouted and turned around. She always felt a little dizzy when she saw her aunt. Blanca looked almost exactly like her mother. The only difference was that her mother had a tiny mole on her right cheek.

"Why would you want to move?" Blanca demanded again. "Why would anyone want to leave their home?"

"So I can go to school," Fina answered. "I asked Señor Vega if we could have a school at the hacienda, but he said no."

Blanca picked up a blouse and began to refold it. "I can teach you how to read and write, Fina. You don't need to go anywhere," she replied.

"That would take too long! We only get to see you three or four times a year," Fina protested. Then she had an idea. "You should come with us, Aunt Blanca!"

Blanca looked at her sister. Neither of them said anything. Fina knew a whole conversation was going on between them. Her mother always said that she and Blanca knew what the other one was thinking. It didn't matter how many miles they lived apart from each other. If they moved to the United States and Blanca stayed in Mexico, would that still be true?

Raul held up hand. "Wait a minute! Wait a minute! Nobody's moving—not yet. We're just thinking about it," he explained. "We were hoping to see you today, Blanca, so we could talk to you about it. If we moved, of course, we would want you to come with us."

"There's nothing to talk about," Blanca said. She reached into her pocket and pulled out a coin. "Here, Fina, go buy yourself some *camote*."

Fina loved the sweet potato candy. It was sticky and sweet, but she didn't want to leave now. Important things were being talked about. She needed to find out what was going to happen.

"No, thank you, Aunt Blanca," Fina said politely. "I'm not hungry. I'll just stay here."

Her mother gave Fina a look. Fina had no choice but to take the coin and leave. She walked away as slowly as she could and listened hard. She thought she heard her father say that Mexico was becoming a dangerous place. Fina turned around to look. Her aunt was fanning herself and looking at her father as if she didn't believe him. A small group of tourists, chatting loudly and laughing, surrounded Fina. She couldn't see her family. She darted out from the group to get her sweet treat.

When Fina returned, Aunt Blanca was gone. Her mother looked sad and angry. Her father did too.

"What happened?" Fina asked. "Where's Aunt Blanca?" No one said a thing. Then suddenly Marcos jumped up and took her hand.

"Come on. Give me a tour of the beautiful city of Puebla. I want you to tell me everything you know about this old city."

Raul pointed to the sun. "Watch the sun," he told them. "Be back in two hours.

As they walked, Marcos told Fina what had happened. Blanca had listened to Raul's reasons for leaving: So Fina could go to school. So they'd be free from men like Señor Vega. So they could own their own land.

Marcos stopped. "I don't know if I should tell you this part," he said.

Fina held her breath. She didn't know whether she wanted Marcos to tell her or not. "Is it about Aunt Blanca?" she asked.

Marcos shook his head. "No. Papa said that one of these things was true. Number one, nothing would ever change in Mexico. Men like Señor Vega would always own the land, and people like us would always work for them. Or, number two, that everything in Mexico was going to change—only nobody knew if the change would be good or bad."

"What does that mean?" Fina asked.

Marcos shrugged. "Some people want to throw out the president. They want to take the land back from men like Señor Vega. They will fight if they have to, and that might start a war."

Fina was quiet for a few seconds. Finally, she asked, "Why did Aunt Blanca leave?"

Marcos paused before speaking. "She said she would not move and that if we did, then she'd never see us again. Aunt Blanca said it was hard enough seeing us only a few times a year, and each time she couldn't stand saying goodbye to us. Then she just left."

Marcos picked up a stone, reared back, and let it go as if he were pitching a baseball. The stone hit a tree a hundred yards away. "You know I want to play baseball the same way you want to go to school," he said quietly.

Fina squeezed her brother's hand. There must be a way to make everyone happy, even Aunt Blanca. Was moving the answer?

FINA'S STORY

A few months later, Fina was sweeping the dirt floor of their house. She heard a horse gallop up outside the house. Then she heard Señor Vega's voice calling, "Raul! Raul Recio!"

What was the *señor* doing here? Why wasn't he in Mexico City?

Looking out the window, Fina saw her mother go to meet him. "Señor Vega!" her mother said. She rubbed her hands nervously on her apron. "How nice to see you! May I offer you some cool water or—"

Señor Vega waved his hand. "No, no, no! Where is your husband?"

"He's repairing a fence, as he was told to do."

The landowner looked around, as if he didn't believe her. "Then where is your son?" he asked.

"He's working in the cornfields, as he does almost every day," she replied.

"Are you sure Marcos isn't in the fields, throwing baseballs at my scarecrows?" Señor Vega asked.

Fina's mother stood up even straighter. "My son is at work in your fields, *señor*. We are good people. We always do what we are told."

Señor Vega waved a fly away from his face. "Well, I'm hearing that many of my workers are unhappy. People in

28

CHANGES AHEAD

Mexico City are talking. They say that the workers want things to change. I am here to tell them that nothing will change. There will be no new president. Do I make myself very clear?"

"Yes, *señor*," her mother said. Fina noticed that her mother looked away as she spoke. She had never done that before. "I'll tell my husband and my son what you said."

"You are all to stay here on my hacienda. I forbid you to go to Puebla. Do you understand me?" Señor Vega demanded.

Her mother nodded her head. Señor Vega flicked the reins and rode away. A cloud of dust hid her mother, but then it cleared. Fina had never seen her mother so angry.

All through the summer and into the fall, the Recios talked about whether they should move to the United States. One thing kept them from leaving: Aunt Blanca. So they made many excuses to stay.

"It's not so bad here," Marcos would say. "Señor Vega has built a very fine baseball field."

"We have food to eat," Fina's mother would say. "We have a fine roof over our heads."

"I'm learning English at the market in Puebla," Fina would say. "I don't need to go to a real school."

"If only we could talk Blanca into going with us," Fina's father would say.

Then her mother would leave the house and go for a long walk by herself.

By early November, they got permission to go to the market again. They packed their goods into the cart and left early in the morning. Much had changed in Puebla. There were soldiers everywhere instead of tourists. The soldiers held rifles tightly in their hands. People crowded the streets. Raul had to search for a place to park the donkey cart. They would have to carry everything by hand to the market in the plaza.

"What's going on?" her mother asked.

"I don't know. But stay close together. You too, Marcos," her father ordered. Fina had never heard her father speak that way. He sounded scared.

More soldiers arrived while the family settled in. "Something's wrong," Marcos murmured. "There must be hundreds of soldiers."

Everyone on the street looked frightened. Fina noticed many people began to pack their wares and were quietly and quickly leaving.

Suddenly the sound of gunfire filled the air. Everyone froze and then began to run. It was chaos.

"Let's go back to the cart!" Fina's father shouted. Her mother bent to pick up blouses. "No, leave them, Teresa." Her mother dropped the blouses and the family ran to their cart.

The gunfire continued. A group of soldiers pushed through the crowd. Fina felt Marcos's hand slipping out of hers. She tried to hold on tight, but he was gone.

"Marcos!" Fina cried. "Marcos, where are you?" There was no answer.

CHAPTER 3

Trouble in Puebla

They waited anxiously at the cart for what seemed like hours. Fina thought that everyone in Puebla must have passed their cart—everyone except Marcos. It was getting late too. But at least the shooting had stopped.

Then two soldiers walked up to them. Fina thought they looked as scared as everyone else did. One of the soldiers tapped the wheels of the cart with his gun. "Get moving! The show's over. Go home," he ordered.

"*Por favor*—please—we're waiting for our son," Raul began. "He—"

The other soldier took hold of the donkey's bridle. "Get going, or we'll throw you all in jail!"

Fina's father looked like he was going to say something, but her mother grabbed his arm. "Let's go," she said quietly. "Marcos will find his way home." They joined the long line of people leaving the city.

Fina sat in the front of the cart between her parents. Raul carefully guided the donkey through the crowd. Fina kept calling her brother's name. If only she had been able to hold on to his hand!

Fina looked around. Everyone looked frightened. People kept their heads down and trudged forward. Finally, Fina could not stand the silence. "Has the war started?" she blurted. Her parents looked at her and then away. Quietly her father asked her where she had heard about the war.

Fina burst into tears as she replied. "Marcos told me that people would fight for their land and there might be a war." Would her family fight Señor Vega to get their family's land back? Were they strong enough to fight him?

Her mother wrapped her arms around Fina. "Ssshh. Help me look for Marcos. Keep calling his name." But neither of her parents denied there was a war. Fina pulled her shawl tighter and called out her brother's name.

As they traveled, they talked to other people on the road who had also been in Puebla. They were finally able to piece together what had happened in the city. Hundreds of soldiers had surrounded a house. People inside the house had been hiding guns. They were going to use the guns to start a war in Mexico. The people inside the house and the soldiers had begun shooting at each other.

The battle had gone on for hours. Finally, the soldiers had killed the three men inside the house and had arrested the three women.

Everyone on the road seemed to know a little piece of the story. But nobody had seen a sixteen-year-old boy named Marcos Recio.

The moon was so bright that Fina could see the snow-covered tip of Popo. Marcos had promised that they would climb the volcano together for her fifteenth birthday. Marcos had promised. That meant he had to be all right. Marcos always kept his promises.

When they got home, their house was dark. They'd all expected to see the glow of a fire. They'd all thought that somehow Marcos would be waiting for them.

Her mother gave a little moan. "We have to go back to Puebla," she said. "We have to find Marcos!" Fina and her father nodded.

Soon they were on their way back to the city. They rode in silence. Fina lay in the back of the cart and looked up at the sky. "Marcos, where are you?" she whispered over and over again.

Suddenly Raul pulled the cart to a stop. "Did you hear that?" he asked.

At first, Fina could only hear her own heart beating. Then she heard a shout in the distance.

"Hey! Hey! Where are you going?"

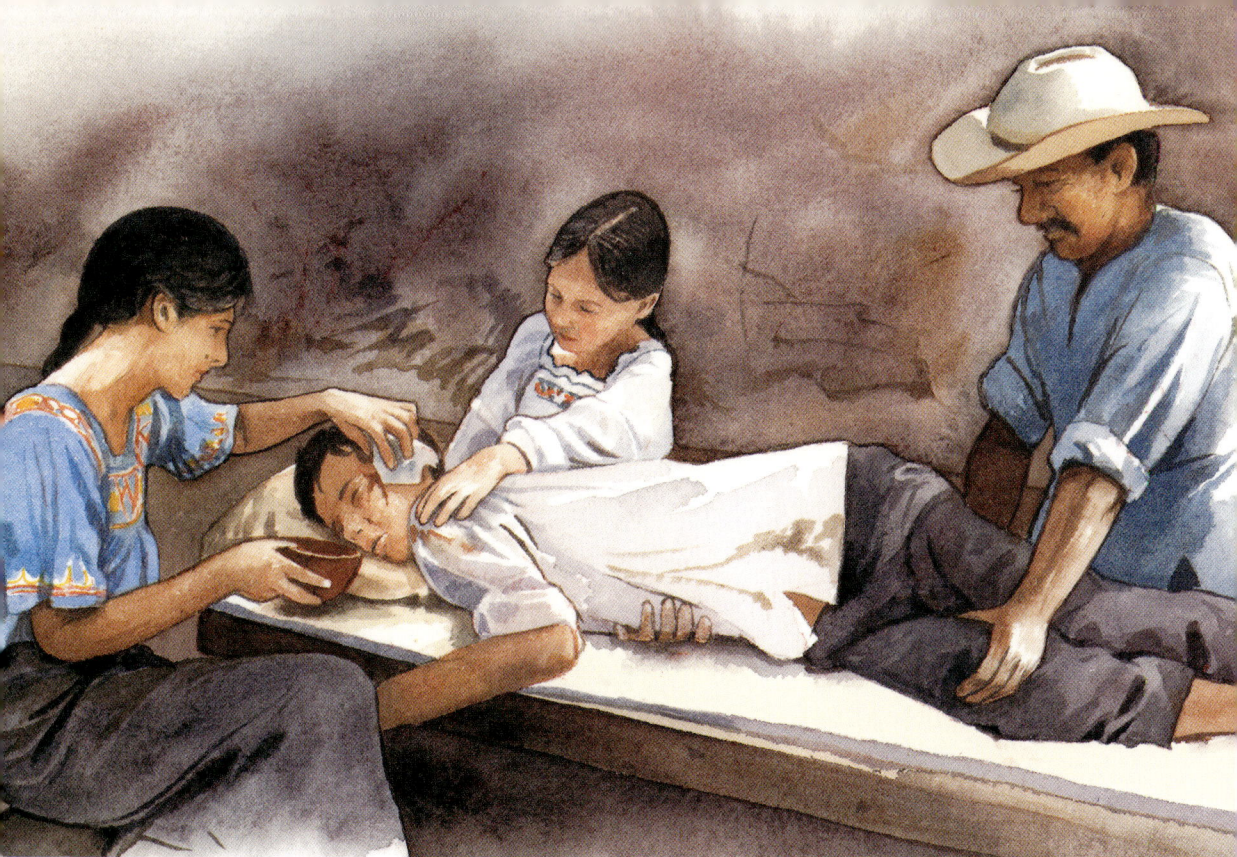

Fina turned around and saw a figure emerging from the bushes and waving his arms. Marcos! She and her mother jumped out of the cart and ran toward him. They hugged each other. Her father shouted for them to get in the cart. They could talk later, once they were safely home.

At home, they stared at Marcos. His clothes were dirty and torn. There was blood on his shirt. He had small cuts on his face. "What happened to you?" his father asked.

But his mother stood up. "First, we must take care of his cuts. Then we'll give him something to eat and drink. Then we're all going to sleep. Tomorrow he can tell us what happened," she said.

Raul nodded his head. "I'll pump some fresh water and build a fire. Fina, would you come and feed Poco?"

Fina followed her father to the door. They both stopped in the doorway and looked back. They wanted to make sure that Marcos was really there. Fina took her father's hand and walked outside with him.

"Do you really think Marcos is all right?" she asked.

"He looks tired. But by tomorrow, I think he'll be fine," he answered.

Fina had so many questions that she didn't know which one to ask next. What had happened in Puebla? Why? Was this the beginning of a war? Was Aunt Blanca all right? Would they ever see her again? Were they really going to move?

The next morning, Marcos told his story: "The crowd kept pushing me back. I couldn't hold on to Fina's hand anymore. I got lost in the crowd. I kept hearing guns firing. It sounded like we were heading right for them. I tried to push my way out of the crowd, but there were too many people. Then, all of sudden, a line of soldiers threw some of us against a wall. People started throwing rocks. The window over our heads broke, and some of the glass cut me. One of the soldiers grabbed me. He looked like he was not much older than me. He said he was going to take me to jail. I kept asking why, but he wouldn't answer. The gunfire got louder and louder. Suddenly, the soldier pushed me away and told me to get out of there, to go home and never come back. I ran and ran, but I couldn't seem to escape. Finally, I dodged down a side street and hid until a group of soldiers passed. Men were throwing rocks at them, and the soldiers were fighting back. When it got dark, I ran toward home. Then I heard someone calling my name. It was the man who runs the store at the hacienda. He had a wagon, the one with the two horses. I jumped in, and we raced out of there. We drove to the hacienda, and I walked home. Every time I heard someone on the road, I hid. I thought it was the soldiers." Marcos turned to his parents. "I don't ever want to go back to Puebla."

"Don't worry, we won't. It's not safe there," his mother said as she wiped his face with a damp cloth.

His father spoke in a soft voice as if he were talking to himself. "But if we don't go, we won't earn any money, and we'll go into **debt**."

"We grow enough food to eat," Teresa told her husband. "We have water. I make our clothes. We have everything we need here."

---

debt – owing money

"No," said her father. He looked around. "It's time that we left."

Her mother rubbed the palm of her hand along the white wall. Then she looked at Marcos and Fina. She nodded and said, "We have to send word to Blanca."

They left the next day. Raul wrapped his tools and some seeds in a blanket. Teresa packed her *comal,* the pan she cooked tortillas on, in a basket. They rolled their clothes in blankets and baskets and put them in the back of the cart.

Raul lifted Fina into the cart. "Wait!" she cried. "The chickens! We have to take the chickens!"

"They don't belong to us. They belong to Señor Vega," her father reminded her. "Someone will be here soon to take them."

Fina took a last look at the house. Then she shut her eyes and fell asleep. When she opened them again, she couldn't see their house anymore.

CHAPTER 4

The Journey

They boarded a train in Mexico City. Fina kept looking back at the crowd. She was sure Aunt Blanca would change her mind about Laredo and suddenly appear. But Fina knew in her heart that it would take a long time for their message to reach Blanca. They had told a friend on their hacienda, who would tell a friend in Puebla, who would tell a friend on Blanca's hacienda.

The inside of the train was packed with passengers. People filled the long wooden benches that ran along either side of the car. Some men and women tried to balance bundles of their belongings on top of their heads. As the train jerked out of the station, the bundles tumbled to the floor. Fina heard the sound of breaking pottery. She hoped it wasn't pieces of beautiful pottery from Puebla. Sadness suddenly filled her. They would never live in a house with tiles now.

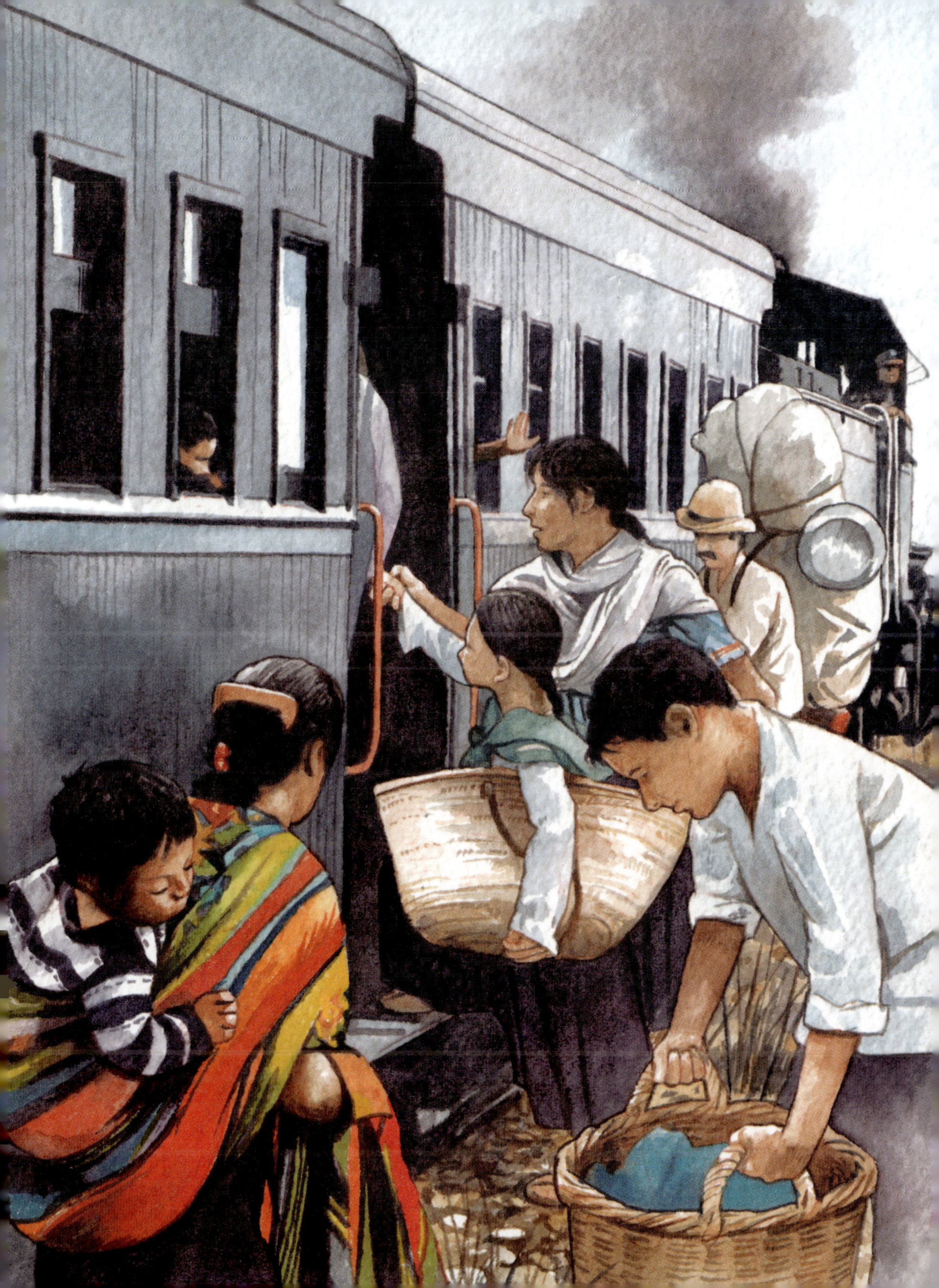

Marcos was standing up, but it looked like he was asleep on his feet. Fina's mother stared straight ahead. She looked like the saddest person in the world. Fina knew she was wishing that Aunt Blanca had come with them. Even if Blanca did hear that they had moved to Laredo, how would she ever find them there?

Fina's father stood in front of her. He looked almost excited as he leaned down to point through the open window. "See how the land is changing, Fina? It's getting flatter."

The land *had* gotten flatter—and drier. It was changing from green to brown. There were fewer trees and bushes, and most of them had sharp thorns. Occasionally, Fina spotted one or two skinny cows through the window. Their horns were long and sharp.

All the windows in the train were open to let in air. But it was still hot inside the car. People's hair and clothes were soon covered with a brown layer of dust. Fina could even taste dust in her mouth. She stuck out her tongue and asked her father, "Is my tongue brown?"

He nodded and stuck out his tongue. It was brown too. "The wind is blowing from the north. We might have dirt from the United States in our mouths."

The way he said it made Fina think that having dust all over her was something special. She wished she could be as excited as her father was.

A woman sitting next to Fina laughed. "Dirt is dirt, no matter where it comes from. Here, this should help." She handed an orange to Fina. "Where are you from? Where are you going?" she asked.

"We used to live outside Puebla, about 15 kilometers south of the city. We're going to Laredo," her father told the woman.

The train stopped. A crowd of people stood near the tracks, waiting to board the train. One man held a goat. Fina thought about their old donkey. He could be mean and stubborn. What if his new owners hurt him or didn't feed him enough? Had Fina left out enough grain for the chickens to eat?

Fina didn't want to think about their donkey or chickens or their home anymore. She listened to her father and the woman talking about Laredo. She was surprised that her father knew so much about the town.

Fina leaned against her mother and took her hand. "Listen to Papa. He knows everything about Laredo," she whispered.

Her mother smiled. It was a sad smile, but it was still a smile. "Your papa is a very smart man."

Tracing lines on her mother's palm, Fina whispered, "After I learn to read and write, I'm going to write to Aunt Blanca. I'm going to talk her into coming to stay with us in Laredo."

FINA'S STORY

Fina hoped it wouldn't take her long to learn all that she needed to know. With her mother's arm around her, she fell asleep.

Late the next afternoon, the train rolled across a steel bridge over the Rio Grande. Her father had told her to watch for this river. When she saw it, he'd said, she would know they were almost there. The river divided Mexico from the United States.

Fina looked back at Mexico and then ahead at the United States. The land on either side of the river looked the same—flat, brown, and dry. There was a city on each side of the river. Nuevo Laredo, Mexico, was on one side. Laredo, Texas, was on the other side. Soon they stopped at the Laredo train station.

It was early November, but Laredo was hot. Like the other train passengers, the Recios went down to the Rio Grande to wash their faces and hands. Then Fina and her

THE JOURNEY

family walked toward the center of the city. An electric trolley car whizzed past them.

"Did you see that?" Fina asked. "Did you see how fast it was going?"

The trolley traveled on tracks just like the train, but the tracks were laid in the middle of the wide street. Some people were walking and riding horses. Others were driving cars and ox carts filled with barrels of water.

Up ahead, Fina could see a brick building with a tall tower. Many of the buildings along the street were made of adobe and had flat roofs, like their house in Mexico. Many of the people around them were speaking Spanish.

Fina took a deep breath. She could smell tortillas being cooked, just like in Mexico. But Laredo smelled different than Puebla did. Fina smelled a river instead of the mountains of home.

"Look!" Marcos said. He pointed toward a grocery store. A poster in its front windows showed a baseball team holding bats and gloves. "Baseball!"

FINA'S STORY

Fina stared through the window. Inside the store, a young woman scooped beans out of a big wooden barrel. She poured the beans into a paper bag.

A voice behind them said, "So you like baseball?"

Both Fina and Marcos jumped. A man with white hair and a white mustache stood behind them. He wore a gray suit with a little black bow tie. Fina stared at the gold ring on his finger. Marcos looked down at his own clothes and tried to brush off some of the dust.

"My brother is the best baseball player in Puebla," Fina informed the man. "He can run. He can hit. He can pitch. He can catch. He can do it all."

The man laughed. "I guess he does like baseball, then."

Marcos tapped the window in front of the poster. "Please, *señor*, where can I try out for this team?"

"Not so fast," his father said. "We need to find work and a place to live."

Fina wandered to the front door of the store and peeked in. Glass jars full of hard candy lined the counter. It looked like one of them held

46

camotes, the sweet potato candy she loved so much. But Fina was sure the candy in the glass jars would taste different than the candy her father used to buy for her at the market in Puebla. This was Laredo, not Puebla.

She reached out and touched the wall. It was made of adobe. She shut her eyes and imagined she was back home in Puebla, touching the wall of their house.

Then Fina smelled a sweet scent, like a flower she'd never smelled before. She opened her eyes. The young woman who had scooped the beans into the paper bag was standing in front of her.

"That's a beautiful blouse you're wearing," she said.

Fina stood up proudly. "My mother made it for me."

The young woman called to the white-haired man, "Daddy, did you see this little girl's blouse? Look at the work. Isn't it beautiful?"

The man seemed to look at Fina for the first time. "Of course, it is. They're from Puebla. Everybody knows that the women of Puebla sew beautifully."

Her mother spoke up. "*Señor,* is there a market here in Laredo? I used to sell my blouses at the market in Puebla."

"*Sí,* the market is every Saturday. Go to that tall building, the one with the tower. That's El Mercado, the market square," the man said.

They thanked him and began to walk away.

"*¡Bienvenido!* Welcome to Laredo!" he called.

Fina ran back to him. She'd almost forgotten the most important question of all. "Please, sir, do you know where I can go to school?"

The man shook his head. "Maybe in a few years there will be a school you can go to," he told Fina.

Their new home was built of sticks. All the homes around them were built of sticks and mud. The houses were called jacales. Sunlight shone through the spaces between the thick sticks. Fina's mother hung striped blankets on the walls to keep some of the light out. The dirt floor wasn't smooth and cool like the dirt floor in their home in Puebla was, but it was their house.

Fina could hear the voices of their neighbors through the walls of the house—and could see them through the cracks in the walls. They were outside, building and tending cooking fires. Someone played a guitar and sang.

Fina's father brought in two buckets of water and set them down. He rubbed his wife's shoulders. "Everything will be all right," he promised.

"How can you say that?" she asked in a low voice. "In two weeks, all of the onions will be planted. There won't be any more work for us until the spring when the onions are ready for harvest. How will we live until then?" Fina didn't want to hear any more bad news.

"I'll help Marcos gather wood," she offered. Her father nodded. Fina slipped out the door and stopped. She suddenly felt shy. In Mexico, their neighbors lived miles away. In Laredo, they were surrounded by people.

The sun would set soon. Fina could see that the land wasn't as flat and as dry as she'd thought it was. Trees and bushes grew along the river. Fina gasped as a huge white bird flew out of the trees. It was beautiful! Seeing the bird made her feel better.

Then her mother's voice came through the cracks in the house. "There's not enough work. The schools are only for the children of rich people. Why did we come here?" she asked.

Fina couldn't catch her breath. Tears slid down her cheeks. Her mother was right. Why had they come? She should be in Puebla right now, feeding the chickens. They were probably starving by now. The donkey's new owner was probably being mean to him. Aunt Blanca was probably crying herself to sleep.

Marcos appeared. He held a few sticks in his hands. They would never be able to start a fire with just a few sticks. Fina began walking toward the river.

"What's wrong? Where are you going?" Marcos called.

"Home!" Fina shouted.

Marcos ran after her and pulled her back. "This *is* our home now," he said gently as she cried.

CHAPTER 5

The Letter

Their first winter in Laredo was hard. By the end of November, there was no more work in the onion fields. Fina's father and Marcos found odd jobs in the city. They swept sidewalks and stores. They unloaded wagons. They did whatever work they could find.

Fina helped her mother dig a garden and plant lettuce and onions. In the spring, they would plant tomatoes, peppers, beans, and maybe corn. Her mother sewed blouses to sell at El Mercado. She taught Fina how to sew.

One morning in December, Fina sat outside their jacal. She was supposed to be sewing a red flower on a small white cotton blouse. Her eyes wandered to their garden. She kept waiting for one of the lettuce seeds to pop out of the dirt. Although they'd watered the garden that morning, the ground already looked dry. How could anything grow here?

THE LETTER

A chicken with shiny brown feathers pecked its way past Fina. It reminded her of the chickens they'd had to leave behind in Puebla. They should have brought the chickens with them. Señor Vega probably didn't even know how many chickens he owned or where they all were. Fina didn't know whether to feel mad or sad. All she knew was that she was tired of being unhappy. She had thought she'd be learning how to read and write, not how to sew.

Fina decided to practice the little bit of English she knew. "*Buenos dias.* Good morning. *¿Como esta?* How are you? *¿Como se llama?* What is your name? *Mi nombre es Josefina Recio.* My name is Josefina Recio," she said out loud.

Then Fina realized a woman standing nearby was listening. The woman held the brown chicken in her arms.

"You speak English," she said, surprised.

"I learned in Puebla, at the market there. I only know those four sentences," Fina confessed.

The woman laughed and said, "That's four more sentences than I know in English."

Teresa appeared in the doorway. "I'm going to gather wood by the river, Fina."

Fina didn't offer to help. She knew that her mother went to the river to be alone. Her mother's eyes would be red when she came back. Fina missed her Aunt Blanca, but her mother missed Blanca much, much more.

The next Saturday, Fina and her mother took the blouses to the market. Her mother had stayed up all night to finish the last blouse. Fina didn't think she'd ever seen her mother look so tired.

Even before they had set out all the blouses, their first customer arrived. The *gringa,* the white woman, asked, "*¿Habla ingles?* Do you speak English?"

Fina waited for her mother to shake her head or say something in Spanish. But her mother kept arranging blouses. She suddenly looked like she couldn't understand either Spanish or English.

The woman held up one of the blouses. Its square neck was stitched with red and black birds. "This is so beautiful," the woman said. *"Esta es tan hermosa. ¿Cuánto cuesta?* How much does it cost?"

Her mother still didn't say anything or even look at the woman.

Fina took a guess. "Seventy *centavos*—I mean seventy cents," she told the woman. She still didn't know the difference between *centavos* and cents. Was a Mexican *centavo* worth more or less than an American cent?

The woman smiled and handed some paper money to Fina. "This is for two blouses—*por dos,*" she said, holding up two fingers.

Fina took the money. There were two bills, and both had ones in each corner. It seemed like too much money, but they didn't have any change to give back. What had her mother and father done in Puebla?

Then Fina remembered the jar of *centavos* that had sat in the corner of their old house. All that money was gone now. How could she explain any of that to this woman?

Before Fina could say anything, the woman began to walk away. *"Muchas gracias!"* she said.

After that, every time someone asked how much a blouse cost, Fina held up one of the bills. Some people walked away. Some people wanted to pay less. They placed American or Mexican coins in the palms of their hands and offered the money. Fina always shook her head firmly and held up the one-dollar bill. By now, she knew

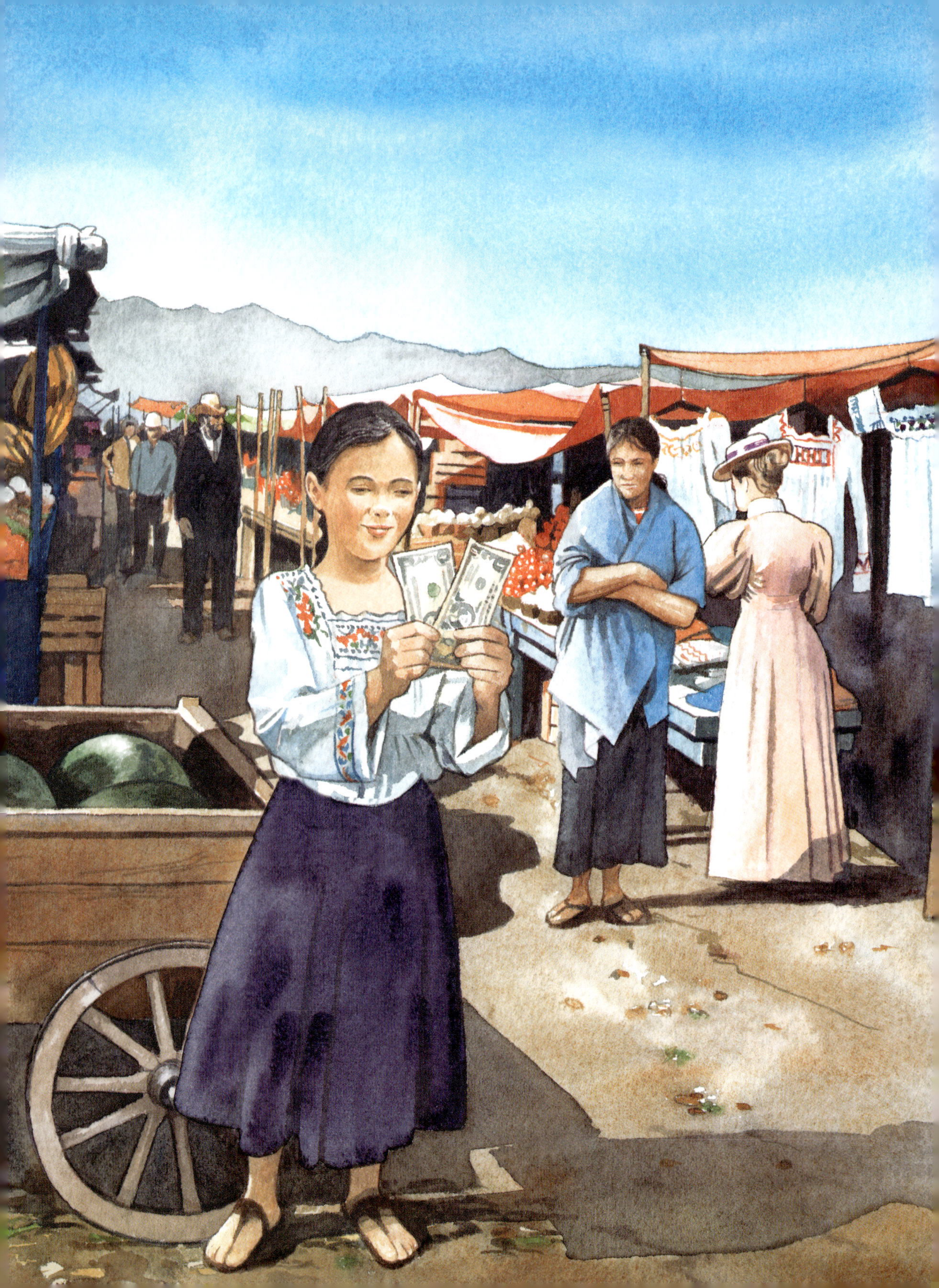

what the paper money was called: one dollar. Some people were happy to pay a dollar for a blouse. Maybe we should charge more, Fina thought.

By noon, they'd sold all the blouses. Her mother hugged her. "What would I do without you, Fina? I was so tired today that I couldn't even think," she said.

The tips of Fina's fingers were sore. All day long, she had pushed and pulled the needle in and out of the white cotton blouse. Her sewing was getting better. She and her mother were working long hours every day. But no matter how fast they sewed, they always sold out of blouses before noon at the market. It seemed like everyone in Laredo knew about her mother's blouses.

Fina did all the talking now. Fina figured she knew over a hundred English words. She was also learning how to spell words in both English and Spanish.

Her parents bought a notebook and a pencil for her. "The market will be your school," her mother explained. "At least for now."

One of their customers wrote down all the letters in the alphabet for her. The man who sold shoes at El Mercado helped her write down words in Spanish and English. Every Saturday, Fina tried to learn at least ten new words.

By March, her father was working in the onion fields again. He always smelled like onions. They'd been in Laredo for five months. The large metal can in their jacal was rapidly filling with dollars and coins. Every night, Raul counted the money. He spoke of buying a building. They would live on the top floor. On the bottom floor, they would run a grocery store.

Marcos talked about trying out for the Laredo Bermudas baseball team in a few weeks. Fina repeated all the English words and facts about Laredo that she'd learned at the market. But her mother never talked about her own dream.

Fina knew what it was—to know that her sister was all right. They'd heard that fights between soldiers and people had broken out in parts of Mexico. Then they'd heard that Mexico had a new president. Would that change anything? Nobody seemed to know yet. But more and more people were coming into Laredo from Mexico.

One night, Fina traced the alphabet on the table, one letter after another. What would her mother want to say to her sister? *Dear Blanca, We arrived safely in Laredo, but we miss you so much.* Suddenly, Fina had an idea. Her mother *could* talk to Blanca again! Fina would write a letter to Blanca for her mother.

THE LETTER

Every Saturday, Fina added a few sentences to the letter to Blanca. She had to be careful because she wanted the letter to be a surprise. She didn't want her mother to feel bad if Blanca didn't write back.

Many people at the market helped Fina. She would tell a customer or the man who sold shoes what she wanted to say. Then she would write it carefully in her notebook, in both Spanish and English. When she was sure she had the spelling correct, Fina would copy the Spanish sentence onto a clean sheet of paper. She worked slowly and carefully so she wouldn't make a mistake.

Finally, on May 15, the letter was finished. Fina wrote, "Much love, from your sister, Teresa, and her family." Her heart was thumping. Her father and Marcos went with Fina to mail it. Now all they had to do was wait.

It took almost three months for Blanca to write back. When the letter arrived, Fina's mother was outside weeding the garden. Her father was adding more brush to the top of the jacal to keep out the hot August sun.

FINA'S STORY

"Surprise, Mama!" Fina said. With a grin she held out a fat envelope.

"What's this?" Teresa asked, wiping her hands on her apron. Then she recognized the handwriting on the envelope. "Blanca! It's from Blanca!" She held the envelope to her chest. Her eyes filled with tears. "But none of us can read it."

THE LETTER

"I can, Mama!" Fina said. Her hands shook as she took the letter. What if she didn't know enough words to read it to her mother? What if she didn't know as much as she thought she did?

Fina began to read slowly. She had to stop a few times to figure out a word, but in the end she was able to read the entire letter to them.

Her mother hugged and kissed Fina. "Blanca's safe!" she said happily.

"And she misses us!" Marcos exclaimed.

"She might even come to visit!" his father added.

Teresa stopped to look at her daughter. "What's wrong, Fina? You have such a funny look on your face."

Fina felt a huge smile spread across her face. "You know what I just realized? I can finally read and write!"

The family stood in the late afternoon sun and thought about just how far they had come to find their new home.

THE FACTS BEHIND THE STORY

Mexico in 1910

Although Fina and her family are fictional characters, this story is based on actual events. For more than thirty years, President Diaz of Mexico took land from farmers and gave it to wealthy landowners. Farm families like Fina's had to work for the new owners. But in 1910, a few leaders began to speak out. Plans were made to force out the president. In November 1910, a battle in the city of Puebla marked the beginning of the Mexican Revolution. Fighting continued for many years.

Laredo, Texas, and Nuevo Laredo, Mexico Laredo was originally a Mexican settlement. But in 1848, the Rio Grande River became the boundary between Mexico and the United States. People who wanted to remain Mexican citizens moved across the river and founded Nuevo Laredo. In the late 1800s, a rail line was built to connect Nuevo Laredo with Mexico City. When the Mexican Revolution began, people traveled north by rail to Laredo to escape the fighting.

Puebla Puebla is Mexico's fourth largest city. It was built by the Spanish in 1531. Puebla has always been an important trading center. Tourists come to see the colorful Talavera tiles made only in Puebla. People buy embroidered blouses in the city's markets. The national dish of Mexico, *mole poblano*, was invented in Puebla. It is a chicken dish made with chocolate and spicy chilis.

Popocatepetl The volcano called Popocatepetl gets its name from two Aztec words: *popoca*, meaning smoke, and *tepetl*, meaning mountain. Popocatepetl has erupted many times in the past 500 years. When experts see signs of an eruption, schools close and people evacuate the area. In 2003, ash from the volcano blew as far as Mexico City.

READ, RESEARCH, AND WRITE

WRITE A PERSONAL LETTER

Imagine that you are Fina writing to Aunt Blanca. What would you tell her about your new life in Laredo? What do you miss most about your old life in Puebla?

- Make a web like the one below.
- In each circle, write about a different experience Fina has had in Laredo.
- Use your completed web to write a letter to Aunt Blanca describing your new life in this city.

There are electric trolley cars.

My life in Laredo

People live in jacales.

EXTEND YOUR READING

READ MORE ABOUT THE SOUTHWEST

Find and read more books about the history of the Southwest. As you read, think about these questions. They will help you understand more about this topic.

- Why do people want to leave the country they live in?
- What problems do immigrants face when they move?
- What has brought settlers to the Southwest?
- How has the Southwest changed over time?

SUGGESTED READING
Reading Expeditions
Travels Across America's Past
The Southwest: Its History and People

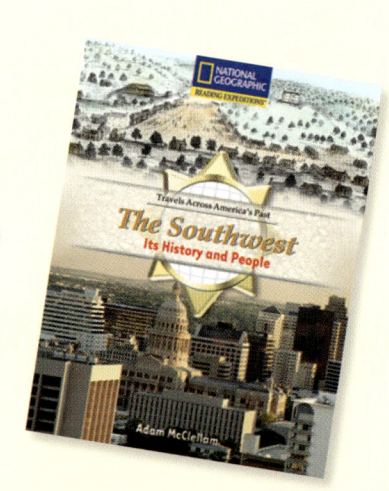